The Man And The Opportunity

Orison Swett Marden

PUSHING TO THE FRONT

CHAPTER I

THE MAN AND THE OPPORTUNITY

No man is born into this world whose work is not born with him.—LOWELL.

Things don't turn up in this world until somebody turns them up.—GARFIELD.

Vigilance in watching opportunity; tact and daring in seizing upon opportunity; force and persistence in crowding opportunity to its utmost of possible achievement—these are the martial virtues which must command success.—AUSTIN PHELPS.

"I will find a way or make one."

There never was a day that did not bring its own opportunity for doing good that never could have been done before, and never can be again.—W. H. BURLEIGH.

"Are you in earnest? Seize this very minute;
What you can do, or dream you can, *begin it*."

"IF we succeed, what will the world say?" asked Captain Berry in delight, when Nelson had explained his carefully formed plan before the battle of the Nile.

"There is no *if* in the case," replied Nelson. "That we shall succeed is certain. Who may live to tell the tale is a very different question." Then, as his captains rose from the council to go to their respective ships, he added: "Before this time to-morrow I shall have gained a peerage or Westminster Abbey." His quick eye and daring spirit saw an opportunity of glorious victory where others saw only probable defeat.

"Is it POSSIBLE to cross the path?" asked Napoleon of the engineers who had been sent to explore the dreaded pass of St. Bernard. "Perhaps," was the hesitating reply, "it is within the limits of *possibility*."

"FORWARD THEN," said the Little Corporal, without heeding their account of apparently insurmountable difficulties. England and Austria laughed in scorn at the idea of transporting across the Alps, where "no wheel had ever rolled, or by any possibility could roll," an army of sixty thousand men, with ponderous artillery, tons of cannon balls and baggage, and all the bulky munitions of war. But the besieged Massena was starving in Genoa, and the victorious Austrians thundered at the gates of Nice, and Napoleon was not the man to fail his former comrades in their hour of peril.

When this "impossible" deed was accomplished, some saw that it might have been done long before. Others excused themselves from encountering such gigantic obstacles by calling them insuperable. Many a commander had possessed the necessary supplies, tools, and rugged soldiers, but lacked the grit and resolution of Bonaparte, who did not shrink from mere difficulties, however great, but out of his very need made and mastered his opportunity.

Grant at New Orleans had just been seriously injured by a fall from his horse, when he received orders to take command at Chattanooga, so sorely beset by the Confederates that its surrender seemed only a question of a few days; for the hills around were all aglow by night with the camp-fires of the enemy, and supplies had been cut off. Though in great pain, he immediately gave directions for his removal to the new scene of action.

On transports up the Mississippi, the Ohio, and one of its tributaries; on a litter borne by horses for many miles through the wilderness; and into the city at last on the shoulders of four men, he was taken to Chattanooga. Things assumed a different aspect immediately. *A master* had arrived who was *equal to the situation*. The army felt the grip of his power. Before he could mount his horse he ordered an advance, and although the enemy contested the ground inch by inch, the surrounding hills were soon held by Union soldiers.

Were these things the result of chance, or were they compelled by the indominable determination of the injured General?

Did things *adjust themselves* when Horatius with two companions held ninety thousand Tuscans at bay until the bridge across the Tiber had been destroyed?—when Leonidas at Thermopylæ checked the mighty march of Xerxes?—when Themistocles, off the coast of Greece, shattered the Persian's Armada?—when Cæsar, finding his army hard pressed, seized spear and buckler, fought while he reorganized his men, and snatched victory from defeat?—when Winkelried gathered to his heart a sheaf of Austrian spears, thus opening a path through which his comrades pressed to freedom?—when for years Napoleon did not lose a single battle in which he was personally engaged?—when Wellington fought in many climes without ever being conquered?—when Ney, on a hundred fields, changed apparent disaster into brilliant triumph?—when Perry left the disabled *Lawrence*, rowed to the *Niagara*, and silenced the British guns?—when Sheridan arrived from Winchester just as the Union retreat was becoming a rout, and turned the tide by riding along the line?—when Sherman, though sorely pressed, signaled his men to hold the fort, and they, knowing that their leader was coming, held it?

History furnishes thousands of examples of men who have seized occasions to accomplish results deemed impossible by those less resolute. Prompt decision and whole-souled action sweep the world before them.

True, there has been but one Napoleon; but, on the other hand, the Alps that oppose the progress of the average American youth are not as high or dangerous as the summits crossed by the great Corsican.

Don't wait for extraordinary opportunities. *Seize common occasions and make them great.*

On the morning of September 6, 1838, a young woman in the Longstone Lighthouse, between England and Scotland, was awakened by shrieks of agony rising above the roar of wind and wave. A storm of unwonted fury was raging, and her parents could not hear the cries; but a telescope showed nine human beings clinging to the windlass of a wrecked vessel whose bow was hanging on the rocks half a mile away. "We can do nothing," said William Darling, the light-keeper. "Ah, yes, we must go to the rescue," exclaimed his daughter, pleading tearfully with both father and mother, until the former replied: "Very well, Grace, I will let you persuade me, though it is against my better judgment." Like a feather in a whirlwind the little boat was tossed on the tumultuous sea, but, borne on the blast that swept the cruel surge, the shrieks of those shipwrecked sailors seemed to change her weak sinews into cords of steel. Strength hitherto unsuspected came from somewhere, and the heroic girl pulled one oar in even time with her father. At length the nine were safely on board. "God bless you; but ye're a bonny English lass," said one poor fellow, as he looked wonderingly upon this marvelous girl, who that day had done a deed which added more to England's glory than the exploits of many of her monarchs.

"If you will let me try, I think I can make something that will do," said a boy who had been employed as a scullion at the mansion of Signor Faliero, as the story is told by George Cary Eggleston. A large company had been invited to a banquet, and just before the hour the confectioner, who had been making a large ornament for the table, sent word that he had spoiled the piece. "You!" exclaimed the head servant, in astonishment; "and who are you?" "I am Antonio

Canova, the grandson of Pisano, the stone-cutter," replied the pale-faced little fellow.

"And pray, what can you do?" asked the major-domo. "I can make you something that will do for the middle of the table, if you'll let me try." The servant was at his wits' end, so he told Antonio to go ahead and see what he could do. Calling for some butter, the scullion quickly molded a large crouching lion, which the admiring major-domo placed upon the table.

Dinner was announced, and many of the most noted merchants, princes, and noblemen of Venice were ushered into the dining-room. Among them were skilled critics of art work. When their eyes fell upon the butter lion, they forgot the purpose for which they had come in their wonder at such a work of genius. They looked at the lion long and carefully, and asked Signor Faliero what great sculptor had been persuaded to waste his skill upon such a temporary material. Faliero could not tell; so he asked the head servant, who brought Antonio before the company.

When the distinguished guests learned that the lion had been made in a short time by a scullion, the dinner was turned into a feast in his honor. The rich host declared that he would pay the boy's expenses under the best masters, and he kept his word. Antonio was not spoiled by his good fortune, but remained at heart the same simple, earnest, faithful boy who had tried so hard to become a good stone-cutter in the shop of Pisano. Some may not have heard how the boy Antonio took advantage of this first great opportunity; but all know of Canova, one of the greatest sculptors of all time.

Weak men wait for opportunities, strong men make them.

"The best men," says E. H. Chapin, "are not those who have waited for chances but who have taken them;

besieged the chance; conquered the chance; and made chance the servitor."

There may not be one chance in a million that you will ever receive unusual aid; but opportunities are often presented which you can improve to good advantage, if you will only *act.*

The lack of opportunity is ever the excuse of a weak, vacillating mind. Opportunities! Every life is full of them. Every lesson in school or college is an opportunity. Every examination is a chance in life. Every patient is an opportunity. Every newspaper article is an opportunity. Every client is an opportunity. Every sermon is an opportunity. Every business transaction is an opportunity,—an opportunity to be polite,—an opportunity to be manly,—an opportunity to be honest,—an opportunity to make friends. Every proof of confidence in you is a great opportunity. Every responsibility thrust upon your strength and your honor is priceless. Existence is the privilege of effort, and when that privilege is met like a man, opportunities to succeed along the line of your aptitude will come faster than you can use them. If a slave like Fred Douglass, who did not even own his body, can elevate himself into an orator, editor, statesman, what ought the poorest white boy to do, who is rich in opportunities compared with Douglass?

It is the idle man, not the great worker, who is always complaining that he has no time or opportunity. Some young men will make more out of the odds and ends of opportunities which many carelessly throw away than other will get out of a whole life-time. Like bees, they extract honey from every flower. Every person they meet, every circumstance of the day, adds something to their store of useful knowledge or personal power.

"There is nobody whom Fortune does not visit once in his life," says a cardinal; "but when she finds he is not ready to receive her, she goes in at the door and out at the window."

Cornelius Vanderbilt saw his opportunity in the steamboat, and determined to identify himself with steam navigation. To the surprise of all his friends, he abandoned his prosperous business and took command of one of the first steamboats launched, at a salary of one thousand dollars a year. Livingston and Fulton had acquired the sole right to navigate New York waters by steam, but Vanderbilt thought the law unconstitutional, and defied it until it was repealed. He soon became a steamboat owner. When the government was paying a large subsidy for carrying the European mails, he offered to carry them free and give better service. His offer was accepted, and in this way he soon built up an enormous freight and passenger traffic.

Foreseeing the great future of railroads in a country like ours, he plunged into railroad enterprises with all his might, laying the foundation for the vast Vanderbilt system of to-day.

Young Philip Armour joined the long caravan of Forty-Niners, and crossed the "Great American Desert" with all his possessions in a prairie schooner drawn by mules. Hard work and steady gains carefully saved in the mines enabled him to start, six years later, in the grain and warehouse business in Milwaukee. In nine years he made five hundred thousand dollars. But he saw his great opportunity in Grant's order, "On to Richmond." One morning in 1864 he knocked at the door of Plankinton, partner in his venture as a pork packer. "I am going to take the next train to New York," said he, "to sell pork 'short.' Grant and Sherman have the rebellion by the throat, and pork will go down to twelve dollars a barrel." This was his opportunity. He went to New York and offered pork in large quantities at forty dollars per barrel. It was eagerly taken. The shrewd Wall

Street speculators laughed at the young Westerner, and told him pork would go to sixty dollars, for the war was not nearly over. Mr. Armour, however, kept on selling, Grant continued to advance. Richmond fell, pork fell with it to twelve dollars a barrel, and Mr. Armour cleared two millions of dollars.

John D. Rockefeller saw his opportunity in petroleum. He could see a large population in this country with very poor lights. Petroleum was plentiful, but the refining process was so crude that the product was inferior, and not wholly safe. Here was Rockefeller's chance. Taking into partnership Samuel Andrews, the porter in a machine shop where both men had worked, he started a single barrel "still" in 1870, using an improved process discovered by his partner. They made a superior grade of oil and prospered rapidly. They admitted a third partner, Mr. Flagler, but Andrews soon became dissatisfied. "What will you take for your interest?" asked Rockefeller. Andrews wrote carelessly on a piece of paper, "One million dollars." Within twenty-four hours Mr. Rockefeller handed him the amount, saying, "Cheaper at one million than ten." In twenty years the business of the little refinery, scarcely worth one thousand dollars for building and apparatus, had grown into the Standard Oil Trust, capitalized at ninety millions of dollars, with stock quoted at 170, giving a market value of one hundred and fifty millions.

These are illustrations of seizing opportunity for the purpose of making money. But fortunately there is a new generation of electricians, of engineers, of scholars, of artists, of authors, and of poets, who find opportunities, thick as thistles, for doing something *nobler than merely amassing riches*. Wealth is not an end to strive for, but an opportunity; not the climax of a man's career, but an incident.

Mrs. Elizabeth Fry, a Quaker lady, saw her oppornity in the prisons of England. From three hundred to four hundred half-naked women, as late as 1813, would often be huddled in a single ward of Newgate, London, awaiting trial. They had neither beds nor bedding, but women, old and young, and little girls, slept in filth and rags on the floor. No one seemed to care for them, and the Government merely furnished food to keep them alive. Mrs. Fry visited Newgate, calmed the howling mob, and told them she wished to establish a school for the young women and the girls, and asked them to select a schoolmistress from their own number. They were amazed, but chose a young woman who had been committed for stealing a watch. In three months these "wild beasts," as they were sometimes called, became harmless and kind. The reform spread until the Government legalized the system, and good women throughout Great Britain became interested in the work of educating and clothing these outcasts. Fourscore years have passed, and her plan has been adopted throughout the civilized world.

A boy in England had been run over by a car, and the bright blood spurted from a severed artery. No one seemed to know what to do until another boy, Astley Cooper, took his handkerchief and stopped the bleeding by pressure above the wound. The praise which he received for thus saving the boy's life encouraging him to become a surgeon, the foremost of his day.

"The time comes to the young surgeon," says Arnold, "when, after long waiting, and patient study and experiment, he is suddenly confronted with his first critical operation. The great surgeon is away. Time is pressing Life and death hang in the balance. Is he equal to the emergency? Can he fill the great surgeon's place, and do his work? If he can, he is the one of all others who is wanted. *His opportunity confronts him.* He and it are face to face. Shall he confess his ignorance and inability, or step into fame and fortune? It is for him to say."

Are you prepared for a great opportunity?

"Hawthorne dined one day with Longfellow," said James T. Fields, "and brought a friend with him from Salem. After dinner the friend said, 'I have been trying to persuade Hawthorne to write a story based upon a legend of Acadia, and still current there,—the legend of a girl who, in the dispersion of the Acadians, was separated from her lover, and passed her life in waiting and seeking for him, and only found him dying in a hospital when both were old.' Longfellow wondered that the legend did not strike the fancy of Hawthorne, and he said to him, 'If you have really made up your mind not to use it for a story, will you let me have it for a poem?' To this Hawthorne consented, and promised, moreover, not to treat the subject in prose till Longfellow had seen what he could do with it in verse. Longfellow seized his opportunity and gave to the world 'Evangeline, or the Exile of the Acadians.'"

Open eyes will discover opportunities everywhere; open ears will never fail to detect the cries of those who are perishing for assistance; open hearts will never want for worthy objects upon which to bestow their gifts; open hands will never lack for noble work to do.

Everybody had noticed the overflow when a solid is immersed in a vessel filled with water, although no one had made use of his knowledge that the body displaces its exact bulk of liquid; but when Archimedes observed the fact, he perceived therein an easy method of finding the cubical contents of objects, however irregular in shape.

Everybody knew how steadily a suspended weight, when moved, sways back and forth until friction and the resistance of the air bring it to rest, yet no one considered this information of the slightest practical importance; but the boy Galileo, as he watched a lamp left swinging by accident in the cathedral at Pisa, saw in the regularity of those oscillations the useful principle of the pendulum. Even the iron doors of a prison were not enough to shut him out from research. He experimented with the straw of his cell, and learned valuable lessons about the relative strength of tubes and rods of equal diameters.

For ages astronomers had been familiar with the rings of Saturn, and regarded them merely as curious exceptions to the supposed law of planetary formation; but Laplace saw that, instead of being exceptions, they are the sole remaining visible evidences of certain stages in the invariable process of star manufacture, and from their mute testimony he added a valuable chapter to the scientific history of Creation.

There was not a sailor in Europe who had not wondered what might lie beyond the Western Ocean, but it remained for Columbus to steer boldly out into an unknown sea and discover a new world.

Innumerable apples had fallen from trees, often hitting heedless men on the head as if to set them thinking, but Newton was the first to realize that they fall to the earth by the same law which holds the planets in their courses and prevents the momentum of all the atoms in the universe from hurling them wildly back to chaos.

Lightning had dazzled the eyes, and thunder had jarred the ears of men since the days of Adam, in the vain attempt to call their attention to the all-pervading and tremendous energy of electricity; but the discharges of Heaven's artillery were seen and heard only by the eye and ear of terror until Franklin, by a simple experiment, proved that lightning is but one manifestation of a resistless yet controllable force, abundant as air and water.

Like many others, these men are considered great, simply because they improved opportunities common to the whole human race. Read the story of any successful man and mark its moral, told thousands of years ago by Solomon: "Seest thou a man diligent in his business? he shall stand before kings." This proverb is well illustrated by the career of the industrious Franklin, for he stood before five kings and dined with two.

He who improves an opportunity sows a seed which will yield fruit in opportunity for himself and others. Every one who has labored honestly in the past has aided to place knowledge and comfort within the reach of a constantly increasing number.

Avenues greater in number, wider in extent, easier of access than ever before existed, stand open to the sober, frugal, energetic and able mechanic, to the educated youth, to the office boy and to the clerk—avenues through which they can reap greater successes than ever before within the reach of these classes in the history of the world. A little while ago there were only three or four professions—now there are fifty. And of trades, where there was one, there are a hundred now.

"What is its name?" asked a visitor in a studio, when shown, among many gods, one whose face was concealed by hair, and which had wings on its feet. "Opportunity," replied the sculptor. "Why is its face hidden?" "Because men seldom know him when he comes to them." "Why has he wings on his feet?" "Because he is soon gone, and once gone, cannot be overtaken."

"Opportunity has hair in front," says a Latin author; "behind she is bald; if you seize her by the forelock, you may hold her, but, if suffered to escape, not Jupiter himself can catch her again."

But what is the best opportunity to him who cannot or will not use it?

"It was my lot," said a shipmaster, "to fall in with the ill-fated steamer *Central America*. The night was closing in, the sea rolling high; but I hailed the crippled steamer and asked if they needed help. 'I am in a sinking condition,' cried Captain Herndon. 'Had you not better send your passengers on board directly?' I asked. 'Will you not lay by me until morning?' replied Captain Herndon. 'I will try,' I answered 'but had you not better send your passengers on board *now?*' 'Lay by me till morning,' again shouted Captain Herndon.

"I tried to lay by him, but at night, such was the heavy roll of the sea, I could not keep my position, and I never saw the steamer again. In an hour and a half after he said, 'Lay by me till morning,' his vessel, with its living freight, went down. The captain and crew and most of the passengers found a grave in the deep."

Captain Herndon appreciated the value of the opportunity he had neglected when it was beyond his reach, but of what avail was the bitterness of his self-reproach when his last moments came? How many lives were sacrificed to his unintelligent hopefulness and indecison! Like him the feeble, the sluggish, and the purposeless too often see no meaning in the happiest occasions, until too late they learn the old lesson that the mill can never grind with the water which has passed.

Such people are always a little too late or a little too early in everything they attempt. "They have three hands apiece," said John B. Gough; "a right hand, a left hand, and a little behindhand." As boys, they were late for school, and unpunctual in their home duties. That is the way the habit is acquired; and now, when responsibility claims them, they think that if they had only gone yesterday they would have obtained the situation, or they can probably get one to-morrow. They remember plenty of chances to make money, or know how to make it some other time than *now;* they see how to improve themselves or help others in the future, but perceive no opportunity in the present. They cannot *seize their opportunity.*

Joe Stoker, rear brakeman on the —— accommodation train, was exceedingly popular with all the railroad men. The passengers liked him, too, for he was eager to please and always ready to answer questions. But he did not realize the full responsibility of his position. He "took the world easy," and occasionally tippled; and if any one remonstrated, he would give one of his brightest smiles, and reply, in such a good-natured way that the friend would think he had overestimated the danger: "Thank you. I'm all right. Don't you worry."

One evening there was a heavy snowstorm, and his train was delayed. Joe complained of extra duties because of the storm, and slyly sipped occasional draughts from a flat bottle. Soon he became quite jolly; but the conductor and engineer of the train were both vigilant and anxious.

Between two stations the train came to a quick halt. The engine had blown out its cylinder head, and an express was due in a few minutes upon the same track. The conductor hurried to the rear car, and ordered Joe back with a red light. The brakeman laughed and said:

"There's no hurry. Wait till I get my overcoat."

The conductor answered gravely, "Don't stop a minute, Joe. The express is due."

"All right," said Joe, smilingly. The conductor then hurried forward to the engine.

But the brakeman did not go at once. He stopped to put on his overcoat. Then he took another sip from the flat bottle to keep the cold out. Then he slowly grasped the lantern and, whistling, moved leisurely down the track.

He had not gone ten paces before he heard the puffing of the express. Then he ran for the curve, but it was too late. In a horrible minute the engine of the express had telescoped the standing train, and the shrieks of the mangled passengers mingled with the hissing escape of steam.

Later on, when they asked for Joe, he had disappeared; but the next day he was found in a barn, delirous, swinging an empty lantern in front of an imaginary train, and crying, "Oh, that I had!"

He was taken home, and afterwards to an asylum, and there is no sadder sound in that sad place than the unceasing moan, "Oh, that I had! Oh, that I had!" of the unfortunate brakeman, whose criminal indulgence brought disaster to many lives.

"Oh, that I had!" or "Oh, that I had not!" is the silent cry of many a man who would give life itself for the opportunity to go back and retrieve some long-past error.

"There are moments," says Dean Alford, "which are worth more than years. We cannot help it. There is no proportion between spaces of time in importance nor in value. A stray, unthought-of five minutes may contain the event of a life. And this all-important moment—who can tell when it will be upon us?"

"What we call a turning-point," says Arnold, "is simply an occasion which sums up and brings to a result previous training. Accidental circumstances are nothing except to men who have been trained to take advantage of them."

The trouble with us is that we are ever looking for a princely chance of acquiring riches, or fame, or worth. We are dazzled by what Emerson calls the "shallow Americanism" of the day. We are expecting mastery without apprenticeship, knowledge without study, and riches by credit.

Young men and women, why stand ye here all the day idle? Was the land all occupied before you were born? Has the earth ceased to yield its increase? Are the seats all taken? the positions all filled? the chances all gone? Are the resources of your country fully developed? Are the secrets of nature all mastered? Is there no way in which you can utilize these passing moments to improve yourself or benefit others? Is the competition of modern existence so fierce that you must be content simply to gain an honest living? Have you received the gift of life in this progressive age, wherein all the experience of the past is garnered for your inspiration, merely that you may increase by one the sum total of purely animal existence?

Born in an age and country in which knowledge and opportunity abound as never before, how can you sit with folded hands, asking God's aid in work for which He has already given you the necessary faculties and strength? Even when the Chosen People supposed their progress checked by the Red Sea, and their leader paused for Divine help, the Lord said, "Wherefore criest thou unto me? Speak unto the children of Israel, *that they go forward.*"

With the world full of work that needs to be done; with human nature so constituted that often a pleasant word or a trifling assistance may stem the tide of disaster for some fellow man, or clear his path to success; with our own faculties so arranged that in honest, earnest, persistent endeavor we find our highest good; and with countless noble examples to encourage us to dare and to do, each moment brings us to the threshold of some new opportunity.

Don't *wait* for your opportunity. *Make it,*—make it as the shepherd-boy Ferguson made his when he calculated the distances of the stars with a handful of glass beads on a string. Make it as George Stephenson made his when he mastered the rules of mathematics with a bit of chalk on the grimy sides of the coal wagons in the mines. Make it, as Napoleon made his in a hundred "impossible" situations. Make it, as *all leaders of men,* in war and in peace, have made their chances of success. Golden opportunities are nothing to laziness, but industry makes the commonest chances golden.

> "There is a tide in the affairs of men,
> Which, taken at the flood, leads on to fortune;
> Omitted, all the voyage of their life
> Is bound in shallows and in miseries;
> And we must take the current when it serves,
> Or lose our ventures."

> "'Tis never offered twice; seize, then, the hour
> When fortune smiles, and duty points the way;
> Nor shrink aside to 'scape the specter fear,
> Nor pause, though pleasure beckon from her bower;
> But bravely bear thee onward to the goal."

CPSIA information can be obtained
at www.ICGtesting.com
Printed in the USA
LVHW101347160720
660870LV00025B/728

9 781169 172609